HAMPSHIRE BUSES

JOHN LAW

AMBERLEY

The author sadly never saw the buses of North Hampshire until the 1970s, and so was unable to photograph the vehicles of Aldershot & District. Fortunately, preservationists saved No. 506 (AAA 506C) and have restored it to its full glory. This 1965-built Dennis Loline with Weymann bodywork is seen at a rally at Netley Park near Southampton.

First published 2017

Amberley Publishing
The Hill, Stroud
Gloucestershire, GL5 4EP

www.amberley-books.com

Copyright © John Law, 2017

The right of John Law to be identified as the Author of this work has been asserted in accordance with the Copyrights, Designs and Patents Act 1988.

ISBN 978 1 4456 6830 7 (print)
ISBN 978 1 4456 6831 4 (ebook)

British Library Cataloguing in Publication Data. A catalogue record for this book is available from the British Library.

Typesetting by Amberley Publishing.
Printed in the UK.

Introduction

In 1974, Hampshire became smaller. Government boundary changes in that year meant that Christchurch and Bournemouth went into Dorset. Nevertheless, Hampshire remains one of England's largest counties. The county town of Winchester was once the capital of England, while two other major cities, Southampton and Portsmouth, dominate the southern coastline and the Solent. Much of Hampshire remains rural, with two of Britain's National Parks within its boundaries – the New Forest and the South Downs. The north of the county has the large and expanding town of Basingstoke, plus Aldershot with its military connections. Between the two extremes are delightful small towns like Alton, Ringwood and Petersfield.

This book covers the buses within the present boundaries of Hampshire. The county's public road transport commenced with the opening of a horse tramway in Portsmouth in 1865. Expansion soon followed and electrification began in the early years of the twentieth century. The nearby city of Southampton began to see horse-hauled trams in 1879, with the network being electrified by 1903. The city's trams survived the severe bombing of the Second World War, but finally succumbed to the will of the politicians in 1949. Portsmouth's trams, however, ceased to operate in 1936 after trolleybuses were introduced two years earlier. The trolleybuses continued to run until the summer of 1963.

Two other tramways are worthy of mention: the Portsdown & Horndean ran between 1902 and 1935, with services passing to Southdown Motor Services, while the Gosport & Fareham system operated from 1878 to 1929. Both lines were under the ownership of the Provincial Tramways Company, who ran various systems, including that of Grimsby in Lincolnshire. After closure of all the tramways, Provincial continued to run buses between Gosport and Fareham until selling out to the National Bus Company in 1970.

Other than the two municipal operators, most of Hampshire's bus services were run by Hants & Dorset Motor Services Ltd. This company began life in 1916, calling itself Bournemouth & District, but rapid expansion soon meant a change of name. The company became jointly owned by the British Automobile Traction Company and the Tilling Group. The Southern Railway became a major shareholder in 1929, with subsequent history ensuring that the company was nationalised before the 1950s.

Hants & Dorset's fleet consisted mainly of Bristol buses bodied by Eastern Coach Works, which were standard throughout Tilling Group companies until their takeover by the National Bus Company (NBC). Neighbouring Wilts & Dorset, whose buses could be seen in Hampshire running in from Salisbury, was also a Tilling Group member and the two companies fell under common management in 1964. Under NBC auspices, the Wilts & Dorset name disappeared, with Hants & Dorset's 'Tilling Green' livery being replaced by the ubiquitous 'Poppy Red'. Provincial also came under the management of Hants & Dorset, but always retained a green colour scheme.

In preparation for sale of the NBC's assets, Hants & Dorset was split into three in 1983, with Wilts & Dorset, Provincial and Hampshire Bus each becoming separate entities. Eventually, Wilts & Dorset became part of the Go Ahead Group, while Hampshire Bus went to Stagecoach and Provincial became part of First Group. That fate also eventually befell the two council-owned operations in Portsmouth and Southampton.

Two former British Electric Traction (BET) businesses also operated in Hampshire. Southdown's smart, green vehicles could be found in Portsmouth and the east of Hampshire, while those of Aldershot & District ran around the town of the same name. Both became part of the NBC in 1969. Southdown operations in Hampshire remained largely unchanged until their sale to the Stagecoach Group in 1989. In 1972, Aldershot & District was merged with a former Tilling Group company, Thames Valley, to form the rather strangely named Alder Valley Services – though there never was a River Alder! Preparations for privatisation saw the business split up, with the Aldershot area operations becoming Alder Valley South, which eventually passed into the hands of Stagecoach.

Another large operator worthy of mention is Solent Blue Line. Owned by former Tilling Group company Southern Vectis, deregulation saw the newly privatised company, which was owned by its management, expand from its natural boundaries of the Isle of Wight. Solent Blue Line began running buses in Southampton in 1987 and soon became a major player. Both Solent Blue Line and Southern Vectis were sold to the Go Ahead Group in 2005 and, renamed Blue Star, many routes around Southampton still operate today.

Despite the dominance of the big companies, several independents ran stage-carriage routes within Hampshire. Perhaps the most famous was King Alfred Motor Services of Winchester, whose green buses could be found there until its takeover by Hants & Dorset in 1973.

Basil Williams, operating under the names of Southern Motorways and Hants & Sussex, once ran several services around his base in Emsworth, using at one point former London GS-type Guy Specials that were later replaced by AEC Merlins, which were also from London. Operations ceased in the 1990s.

From 1986, deregulation and the tendering process for rural bus services saw several independent companies running stage services in Hampshire. A good proportion, such as Xelabus, Emsworth & District and Brijan Tours, continue in business today, but others, such as Velvet, Countryliner and Countywide, have vanished.

Nevertheless, Hampshire remains a county worthy of a visit by Britain's bus enthusiasts. This book portrays what is still present today and those vehicles that once operated bus services in the past.

Finally, thanks are due to 'Bus Lists on the Web' for providing much assistance during the preparation of this book.

We start this book of Hampshire's buses with a look at a long-vanished, but fondly remembered independent – King Alfred Motor Services of Winchester. The author first visited that city in 1973, just after the takeover by Hants & Dorset. For many years after, King Alfred buses were commemorated every New Year's Day when preserved buses from the Winchester area took over the city's local services. The oldest vehicle preserved by the Friends of King Alfred Buses (FoKAB) group is OU 9286, a 1931 Dennis with eighteen-seat short bodywork, which is seen on the Broadway in the city centre on 1 January 1995. Photograph by Jim Sambrooks.

Built in 1959, this Leyland Tiger Cub, registered WCG 104 and in the custody of FoKAB, is seen on New Year's Day in 1986, at the point on Broadway where it would have been seen twenty years earlier. MCW forty-five-seat bodywork is fitted.

In 1973, during the author's first visit to Winchester, an elderly Hants & Dorset Bristol KSW5G, built in 1952, with 'lowbridge' ECW bodywork, No. 371 (HMW 448), is seen. It had been new to Wilts & Dorset, a fellow former Tilling operator. It is seen overtaking No. 2699 (UOU 419H), a fifty-two-seat Leyland Panther bodied by Plaxton still retaining its King Alfred colours. FoKAB has preserved two vehicles from this batch.

Unusually, King Alfred Motor Services purchased three Metro-Scania single-deck buses in 1971. Seating forty-seven passengers and delivered with a dual-doorway layout, the bus is seen in Broadway, Winchester, loading up for a local journey in 1973. Having just been taken over by Hants & Dorset, AOU 108J has been allocated fleet number 2601. These vehicles, being non-standard in most National Bus Company fleets, were soon transferred to London Country Bus Services, where they joined similar buses on 'Superbus' duties in Stevenage, Hertfordshire.

Former King Alfred Motor Services buses soon began appearing in standard NBC red with Hants & Dorset fleet names. Sometime around 1975, 595 LCG is seen inside Winchester depot, having been given fleet number 2211. This AEC Renown with Park Royal seventy-five-seat bodywork had been new to King Alfred in 1964. The Marston's Bitter advert is a reminder that the Burton-on-Trent brewer had a major presence in Winchester following the takeover of the Hyde Brewery in the city.

One night in 1974, Hants & Dorset No. 2702 (SCG 856) is seen in the depot yard at Winchester. This Weymann-bodied Leyland Tiger Cub, to dual-purpose specification and seating forty-one passengers, had been new to King Alfred Motor Services in 1957.

In 1962, King Alfred Motor Services took delivery of three Leyland Leopards with fifty-three-seat Willowbrook bodies. One of these, registered 413 FOR, is seen with Hants & Dorset as fleet number 2652 on Broadway, Winchester, around 1975.

Former Tilling Group operator Wilts & Dorset had been merged with Hants & Dorset under the auspices of the National Bus Company in 1972. From the former business, fleet number 420 (NHR 909), a Bristol LD6G/ECW sixty-seater fitted with platform doors, is seen in Basingstoke depot yard, around 1975. It had been new to Wilts & Dorset as No. 619 in 1956.

Another vehicle inherited from Wilts & Dorset was OAM 366, which is seen in 1974 as Hants & Dorset No. 792. Carrying both fleet names in NBC and in Tilling style, this Bristol LS5G, built in 1956, has ECW forty-one-seat bodywork. It is photographed in the bus station at Andover.

Also at Andover in 1974 is Hants & Dorset No. 503 (LMR 735F). This too had been new to Wilts & Dorset, where it carried fleet number 815. It is a most unusual bus for a former Tilling fleet, being a Bedford VAM70 with a dual-door, forty-seat Willowbrook body.

New to Hants & Dorset in 1969, No. 3027 (REL 744H) is seen at Gosport bus station in 1974, still in its old livery, but with NBC fleet names. It is a Bristol LH6L with ECW bodywork capable of seating thirty-nine passengers and, unusually, is fitted with dual doorways.

No. 1820 in the Hants & Dorset fleet, registered 6229 EL, had been new in 1960 as No. 874, a thirty-seat Bristol MW6G/ECW coach. By 1974, when photographed in Fareham, it had been relegated to bus duties and given dual-purpose colours in NBC style.

This Hants & Dorset Bristol MW5G with ECW forty-three-seat bodywork had been new as fleet number 814 (2716 EL) in 1959, but a 1971 renumbering saw it become No. 1813. As such, it is seen at Basingstoke bus station around 1975.

A long-lived vehicle in the Hants & Dorset fleet was registered BOW 169. New to the company in 1938, this Bristol L5G originally carried a Beadle body. It was rebuilt in 1944 and given bodywork by ECW. In 1952 it was transferred to Wilts & Dorset and was later cut down to become a towing vehicle. Still bearing evidence of its previous owner, it is seen with Hants & Dorset at Basingstoke around 1975. Behind is an engineless Bristol Lodekka from Eastern National. BOW 169 later went into preservation.

An unusual coach in the Hants & Dorset fleet was this 1963-built Leyland Leopard, No. 3092 (162 AUF). That registration will tell many enthusiasts that the vehicle had been new to Southdown, where it was No. 1162. Weymann Fanfare bodywork is carried, and it is seen in NBC dual-purpose colours in Basingstoke bus station around 1975. Alongside is 327 CAA, a Bedford SB3 built in 1961 with forty-one-seat Harrington coachwork, which operated with Porter's Coaches of Dummer. It had been new to famous Winchester operator King Alfred Motor Services.

Vehicle No. 894 (AEL 2B) was delivered to Hants & Dorset in 1964. This Bristol MW6G with ECW thirty-nine-seat coach bodywork was intended for summer touring duties and was still in use on such operations at Southampton coach station when photographed in 1975. By this time it had been renumbered to become No. 1008. It was withdrawn later in the same year, but had a long life and passed into preservation.

In 1976, its last year of service, Hants & Dorset No. 1118 (5680 EL) is seen in Blechynden Terrace, Southampton, close to the city's Central railway station. Delivered to the company as fleet number 1453, this Bristol FS6G with sixty-seat ECW bodywork was new in 1961. Rear platform doors were fitted as standard to many Hants & Dorset buses and can be clearly seen in this photograph.

A non-standard single-deck bus in the Hants & Dorset fleet was No. 1699 (JKK 194E), which had been new as a forty-five-seater to Maidstone & District. One of several purchased by Hants & Dorset in the early 1970s, this Leyland Leopard/Willowbrook bus was re-fitted with forty-nine places for seated passengers. It is seen in the company's Southampton yard in 1977. After withdrawal the bus was exported to Ireland for further use.

As part of the National Bus Company's 'Market Analysis Project' (MAP) in the early 1980s, local identities were introduced to many constituent fleets, including Hants & Dorset. 'South Hants' stickers have been applied to fleet number 1637 (TRU 219J), a Bristol RELL6G with dual-doorway ECW bodywork capable of seating forty-five passengers. It is seen at Bishops Waltham outstation in 1982.

Bearing 'Provincial' stickers as well as Hants & Dorset's red livery and identity, No. 3556 (GLJ 488N) is seen at Provincial's Hoeford depot (between Gosport and Fareham) in 1981. The bus is a 1975-built Bristol LH6L with forty-three-seat ECW bodywork. The story of the Provincial fleet is told elsewhere within these pages.

In 1983, the Hants & Dorset empire was split up in preparation for privatisation and deregulation. Hampshire Bus took over most of the services within much of the county. Standard NBC red livery was applied in the early years, as demonstrated by No. 3440 (KRU 840W), a Bristol VRT/SL3/6LXB with seventy-four-seat ECW bodywork. It is seen near King Alfred's statue in central Winchester, in March 1984.

Also in Winchester, at the Hampshire Bus combined depot and passenger terminal, we see Leyland National No. 3683 (PJT 260R) in March 1984. This forty-one-seat vehicle had been delivered new to Hants & Dorset in early 1977.

The DMS type of Daimler/Leyland Fleetline built for London Transport did not find favour in the nation's capital and the buses were soon sold on for use elsewhere. By March 1984, when this photograph was taken, OJD 245R (DMS 2245 in its London days) had become No. 1926 in the Hampshire Bus fleet. Seen outside Southampton Central station, this Leyland Fleetline/MCW vehicle had been converted to single-door configuration. It was later sold for further service in Carlisle with Cumberland Motor Services.

Another second-hand vehicle in the Hampshire Bus fleet was No. 176 (XBW 76M), a Bristol RELH6L/Plaxton Elite Express coach, which was new in 1973 to City of Oxford Motor Services. It is seen at the Hard Interchange, Portsmouth Harbour, in early 1984.

It is still the early months of 1984 when Hampshire Bus No. 3626 emerges out of the company's Winchester facilities. Registered NPD 110L, this Leyland National had been intended for use by London Country, but had been hired to Nottingham City Transport from new in 1972. It was eventually sent to London Country's Reigate HQ in 1973, but was never used, as it was quickly swapped for one of Hants & Dorset's Metro-Scania saloons that had been inherited from King Alfred.

The mid-1980s saw Hampshire Bus introduce a new livery, as seen applied to fleet number 3686 (PJT 263R), a forty-nine-seat Leyland National. It had been new to Hants & Dorset in 1976. The bus is seen in Above Bar Street, Southampton, in the summer of 1986.

Above: Hampshire Bus used this fine AEC Matador, which had been heavily rebuilt, as a towing vehicle in case of breakdowns. It is seen inside Southampton depot in the summer of 1986, registered Q910 FRU.

Below: Like many NBC operators, Hampshire Bus was not immune to the preference for minibuses, though not that many were purchased. Ford Transit sixteen-seater No. 20 (C220 XRU) was found outside Southampton depot in the summer of 1987.

On a beautifully sunny spring day in 1987, Hampshire Bus No. 3344 (NEL 118P) is seen at Romsey's small bus station. Fitted with seventy coach seats, this Bristol VRT/SL3/501, bodied by ECW, had been new to Hants & Dorset in 1976.

The forecourt of the Hampshire Bus depot in Southampton was used as a coach station, frequented by a variety of operators. A resident, however, was No. 3061 (SRU 146R), which is seen here bearing 'Hampshire Coach' identity. This 1977-built Leyland Leopard/Plaxton forty-nine-seat coach was photographed here in the summer of 1986.

In the summer of 1987, the new livery of Hampshire Bus is seen applied to a pair of double-deckers in central Southampton. On the left is a standard Leyland Olympian, No. 201 (A201 MEL), new to the company in 1984. More prominent in the photograph is No. 1936 (NAK 418R), a very rare Volvo Ailsa B55 with Van Hool McArdle dual-doorway bodywork. This had been one of a batch delivered to South Yorkshire Passenger Transport in 1977.

Hampshire Bus No. 3850 (AFB 586V) is also seen in Southampton, this time in September 1987. This forty-three-seat Bristol LH6L/ECW saloon had been new to the Bristol Omnibus Company in early 1980.

Pilgrim Coaches was set up to take over the National Bus Company's Southampton-based coaching operations in the run-up to privatisation. At the depot-cum-coach station in Southampton is No. 18 (418 UMX), photographed in the summer of 1986. This Leyland Leopard coach had been new to North Western Road Car as SJA 409K in 1971, but had later been re-bodied by Plaxton, using that company's 'Supreme' style. The rebuild saw it become HBP 333X, but is seen here with its 'cherished' registration.

At the same location and on the same occasion as above, we see Pilgrim Coaches No. 94 (YEL 94Y). This ECW-bodied, fifty-three-seat Leyland Leopard coach had been new to Hants & Dorset in 1982.

An unusual vehicle in the Pilgrim Coaches fleet, No. 2A (A980 XOK) was a Ford Transit with sixteen-seat Carlyle bodywork based on a Dormobile frame. It was, presumably, used on feeder duties, as it would have been unlikely to be heading for Paris when photographed at Southampton in summer 1986. This minibus had been new to Shamrock & Rambler, the Bournemouth-based coaching company owned by the National Bus Company.

A genuine Shamrock & Rambler coach, still in its pre-NBC livery, is seen at Hants & Dorset's main Southampton depot around 1975. Given fleet number 494, SRU 252H is a Bedford VAL70 with Duple Viceroy forty-nine-seat coachwork.

A Shamrock & Rambler coach in National white livery, No. 4114 (ORU 289M) is another visitor to Southampton's coach station, sometime in 1975. Unlike most vehicles used on National Express services, this is a Bedford YRQ, built in 1974. Duple Dominant forty-one-seat coachwork is carried.

The advantage of having one livery for all National Express services is clear, as vehicles can be used from any part of the country. Here is a good example as Milton Keynes City Bus No. 1175 (CHX 175X) is being used for a service to London in summer 1986, seen at the Hard in Portsmouth. This Leyland Leopard with an ECW forty-nine-seat coach body had been new to United Counties in 1982.

Hampshire Buses was sold to Stagecoach in April 1987, though the Southampton area operations were passed on to Solent Blue Line in October of that year. We will visit Solent Blue Line later within these pages, but before that it is appropriate to take a look at the Hampshire Bus vehicles bearing Stagecoach identity. Wearing its newly acquired stripes is Hampshire Bus No. 34 (D934 EBP), a Fiat/Iveco 49.10 minibus with Robin Hood twenty-one-seat bodywork. New in late 1986, it is seen in Andover town centre in April 1990.

On the same occasion as the above photograph, Stagecoach Hampshire Bus No. 723 (TEL 489R) is attracting a good load in Andover. Originally fitted with dual-purpose seating, this Leyland National had been new to Hants & Dorset as fleet number 3723 in 1977.

Above: Also in Andover in April 1990 we see Stagecoach Hampshire Bus No. 207. Registered G807 RTS, it had been new to the company in the summer of 1989. Fitted with eighty-two coach seats, this Alexander-bodied Leyland Olympian is picking up passengers for the medium-distance journey to Winchester.

Below: An unusual bus that had been new to Stagecoach Hampshire Bus was No. 801 (F135 SPX). Named *King Arthur*, it is appropriately seen in Winchester bus station on a local service to Teg Down in summer 1990. This Dennis Javelin with sixty-three-seat Duple 300 bodywork had arrived with the company in March 1989.

The registration 406 DCD had originally been allocated to one of Southdown's famous 'Queen Mary' Leyland Titan PD3 double-deckers. However, it is seen here applied to Stagecoach Coastline (who took over Southdown in East Hampshire) No. 436, arriving in Havant bus station in 2000. Earlier that year, this Dennis Dart/Plaxton saloon had arrived from Hong Kong, where it had operated for Citybus since being new in 1995. Operation in Hong Kong meant that it required fitting with air conditioning, which was retained by Stagecoach and would have been much appreciated on the hot August day when the photograph was taken.

Another view at Havant bus station, this time in March 2003, as Stagecoach's N397 LPN arrives on the long 700 route from Portsmouth to Brighton. By this time the new corporate livery had been applied and the national fleet-numbering system had been instigated. Now carrying No. 16397 as its identity, this coach-seated Volvo Olympian/Alexander double-decker had been new to Stagecoach Coastline as fleet number 397 in 1996.

Not yet given its five-figure national fleet number, Stagecoach 648 (R648 HCD) is seen among the modern buildings of Basingstoke in summer 2002. This Volvo B10M-55 saloon, new in 1998, has forty-eight-seat bodywork by Plaxton to the old Northern Counties 'Paladin' design.

Another import by Stagecoach from Hong Kong, this Volvo B6LE-53/Alexander saloon was new to Citybus in 1997 and was bought for use in the United Kingdom in 2000, becoming Stagecoach No. 43 (R122 NPN). Fitted with air conditioning, it is seen arriving in Havant bus station in March 2003. It was later transferred to the Warwickshire operations and ended up with Manchester area independent Bluebird.

On loan to Stagecoach from Hampshire County Council for its 'Cango' rural operations, Optare Solo YA02 YRO is seen arriving at Havant bus station in March 2003. Under the Stagecoach national numbering scheme, it was allocated fleet number 47040. It was later sold to a Scottish operator in the Stirling area.

With Stagecoach operating the South West Trains rail franchise throughout much of Hampshire and elsewhere, it made sense to integrate some rail and road operations. An innovative scheme was the Petersfield TaxiBus, using a small fleet of Mercedes-Benz 110Cdi eight-seat minibuses. Two of these (with SW03 OYB leading) are seen at Petersfield station, charging only £1 per passenger, in December 2004. The Petersfield operations did not last long and the vehicles were transferred elsewhere.

Another Stagecoach bus-rail scheme was that connecting Petersfield railway station with Waterlooville, a sizeable community that never had a station on the rail network. In a dedicated livery for those duties is NFX 667. New to Stagecoach in 1994 as L607 TDY, this Volvo B10M-55 with Alexander PS bodywork, originally to dual-purpose specification, was allocated fleet number 607 when it started life with the Stagecoach South Coast operations. It is seen in Petersfield on 11 September 2008.

Yet another service connecting rail and road was the X66, which ran between the railway stations at Winchester and Romsey. At the former, Stagecoach No. 32453 (YLJ 332) is seen outside the railway facility in its dedicated livery on 17 August 2007. This Alexander-bodied Dennis Dart had been delivered new to the South Coast operations in 1996 as No. 453 (N453 PAP).

Above: Another vehicle purchased new by Stagecoach South Coast in 1996 was No. 356, which is photographed here after renumbering as 16356 (N356 MPN). This Volvo Olympian with Alexander R-type bodywork, fitted with seventy-five high-back coach seats, is seen in the later Stagecoach corporate colours in Petersfield on 11 September 2008.

Below: Bearing 'Jazz 5' logos for a Basingstoke local route, Stagecoach No. 34633 (GX54 DWC) is seen outside the railway station on 12 May 2010. Very much a standard vehicle within the Stagecoach Group, it is a thirty-eight-seat Dennis Dart SLF bodied by Plaxton.

Park and Ride services in Winchester, operated by Stagecoach on behalf of the City Council, are given a smart two-tone green livery, as worn by No. 27619 (GX10 HCG). This Alexander Dennis Enviro forty-five-seat saloon is seen on the corner of Eastgate Street and the Broadway, in the city centre, on 23 October 2014.

Another Alexander Dennis Enviro saloon, this one with a seating capacity of an additional passenger, is seen outside the Wetherspoon's pub in Edinburgh Road, central Portsmouth, on the previous day to the above photograph. New in the previous year, No. 27875 (GX13 AOV) is dedicated to local routes 20 and 21.

When Wilts & Dorset was split from Hants & Dorset in 1983, the company's red livery was retained, gradually transforming into this smart colour scheme applied to No. 3922 (A174 VFM). New to Crosville as fleet number DOG174, this Leyland Olympian/ECW double-decker is seen on the limited-stop X3 Salisbury to Bournemouth and Poole service in October 2000 at Ringwood. Though Salisbury is in Wiltshire and Bournemouth is now in Dorset, Ringwood is still very much in Hampshire.

Route 65, between Eastleigh and West Wellow, via Romsey, was operated by Wilts & Dorset. In March 2006, No. 3504 (L504 AJT) was on this service as it was photographed arriving at Eastleigh's bus station. This smart DAF SB220 with Optare Delta forty-eight-seat bodywork had been new to the company in 1993. Route 65 has since been cut back to run only as far as Romsey and is today in the hands of another Go Ahead subsidiary, Blue Star.

Wilts & Dorset, after several years of independence under a management buyout, was sold to the Go Ahead Group in 2003. Although the company operates mainly throughout the counties implied by the fleet name, a depot is maintained at Lymington, in Hampshire. It is here that we see No. 739 (K739 DDL), a Northern Counties-bodied Leyland Olympian, on 11 May 2010. This bus had been new to fellow Go Ahead subsidiary Southern Vectis, the main bus service supplier on the Isle of Wight.

Provincial was the name displayed on the buses of the Gosport & Fareham Omnibus Company, which took over operations between those two towns after the Provincial trams ceased in 1929. As an independent company, a fascinating fleet of buses was maintained and this preserved vehicle is a good example. Carrying the lovely Provincial green livery, No. 35 (BOR 767), a 1936-built AEC Regent I with fifty-six-seat Park Royal bodywork, is seen attending a rally at Netley Park near Southampton in summer 1989.

Provincial ceased to be an independent in 1970 when the National Bus Company took over, coming under the wing of Hants & Dorset. Just after the purchase, the late Les Flint visited Gosport bus station and found Nos 21 and 25 (FCR 442 and FCR 445) on service. Both of these Guy Arab III/Park Royal double-deckers had been built in 1948 for Southampton Corporation as Nos 141 and 144.

By 30 June 1971, when Les Flint again found himself in Gosport, the Provincial fleet had been modernised somewhat, with buses drafted in from other NBC organisations. Looking smart in its new livery is No. 34 (XNU 421), a Bristol LS6G/ECW forty-three-seat dual-purpose vehicle. It had been new to Midland General in 1955.

Just prior to the NBC takeover, Provincial ordered several single-deck buses to replace the ageing Guy Arabs. One of these was No. 52 (RAA 20G), which was delivered in March 1969. Photographed after it had been repainted in standard NBC green, around 1974, this Seddon Pennine IV, with dual-doored forty-seat Seddon bodywork, is seen on service in Gosport bus station.

Provincial also received some 1968-built, Strachans-bodied Seddon Pennine IV saloons, such as No. 45 (MHO 194F). Another dual-doored forty-seater, the bus is seen at Gosport's bus station in 1977, by the ferry terminal for Portsmouth. Being non-standard within the National Bus Company, the Seddons were withdrawn soon afterwards.

Another import from a fellow NBC operator into the Provincial fleet was No. 29 (105 CUF), a 1963-built Leyland Leopard/Marshall saloon, which had been new to Southdown. Here it is departing from Gosport bus station, around 1975.

The mid-1970s saw the Leyland National quickly become the standard bus in the small Provincial fleet. An early example was No. 22 (PCG 922M), a forty-four-seat bus with dual doorway. It is seen in Fareham, with a Seddon behind, around 1975.

No. 62 in the Provincial fleet was quite an unusual vehicle in an NBC fleet. Registered HAM 504E, it had been new to Wilts & Dorset in 1967. This Bedford VAM14 with Duple forty-one-seat coachwork is seen at Provincial's Hoeford depot in dual-purpose colours sometime around 1975.

An even more unlikely bus to bear the Provincial name was driver-training vehicle T1 (HWO 344). It is seen slightly out of Provincial's normal operating area at the Southampton depot of Hants & Dorset in 1974.This lowbridge Guy Arab III with Duple bodywork had been new to Welsh operator Red & White in 1950.

To celebrate the centenary of the Gosport & Fareham Company, Provincial's No. 10 (ECG 110K) was temporarily numbered 100 and painted into the old-style colour scheme. This forty-four-seat, dual-doorway Bristol RELL6G/ECW saloon had been ordered by Northern General but was diverted to Provincial. It is seen in Gosport bus station on a sunny day in 1981.

In preparation for privatisation, Provincial No. 2 (A302 KJT) has received a non-standard fleet name as seen as it is loading up in Gosport bus station in summer 1986. This Leyland National Mk 2 had been new two years earlier and was fitted with forty-seven high-backed seats, hence the dual-purpose green and white livery.

The late 1980s saw the Gosport & Fareham Omnibus Company sold to its management to become People's Provincial, with services expanding into other parts of southern Hampshire. In October 1992, when this photograph was taken, the fleet was still very much dominated by the Leyland National. Seen in Southampton city centre, fleet number 64 (KDW 338P) had been new as a standard forty-nine-seater for Western Welsh.

Another second-hand Leyland National to receive People's Provincial's smart colours was No. 23 (RUF 37R). This forty-four-seat, dual-doored bus had been new to Southdown in 1977. It is seen in Gosport bus station having a well-earned rest in March 1993.

A unique vehicle to enter the People's Provincial fleet was No. 333 (H523 CTR). This rare ACE Cougar V with Hampshire-built Wadham Stringer forty-one-seat bodywork had been new as No. 3 in 1990. Not often seen out on the road, the photographer was lucky to find it at Hoeford depot in March 1993.

Competition saw People's Provincial operating Portsmouth local services and it is at the Hard Interchange, beside the rail and ferry terminals, that No. 591 (NFX 130P) is seen in autumn 1995. This Alexander-bodied Daimler Fleetline, convertible to open-top, had been new to Bournemouth Transport in 1976. People's Provincial was later taken over and absorbed into First Bus, whose activities we will look at later in this publication.

The North Hampshire town of Aldershot, known for its military connections, was originally served by Aldershot & District, which combined with Thames Valley Omnibus Company to form NBC subsidiary Alder Valley. Its operations were mainly in Surrey and Berkshire, but Aldershot's town services were maintained by a fleet of minibuses. On a freezing and misty morning in early 1988, No. 479 (E203 EPB), an Iveco 49.10 with twenty-five-seat Robin Hood bodywork, is seen in the town's small bus station.

On the same occasion as above is Alder Valley No. 340 (D340 WPE), a smaller minibus seating just sixteen passengers in a Ford Transit adapted for passenger use by Carlyle. The legal lettering reads 'Alder Valley South', reflecting the split-up of the company prior to privatisation. The year 1992 saw the Hampshire operations sold to the Stagecoach Group.

The vehicles of Western National's coaching arm, Royal Blue, were frequent visitors to Hampshire's coastal towns and cities. Seen parked in Portsmouth sometime around 1972 is fleet number 2268 (57 GUO). This 1961-built Bristol MW6G with ECW thirty-nine-seat coach bodywork still wears its pre-NBC colours, while the younger Bristol MW behind is in the later, mainly white, livery.

Royal Blue coaches were regularly seen at Southampton's coach station and No. 1308 (RDV 443H) was photographed there around 1977. The vehicle is a Bristol LH6L with Duple coachwork seating forty-one-passengers. Royal Blue operations were soon absorbed into those of National Express.

The green buses of Southdown were regular visitors to Portsmouth and the surrounding areas of East Hampshire. The company's main depot in the city was at Hilsea, north of the centre, but a nondescript building and coaching yard existed closer to Portsmouth & Southsea railway station at Hyde Park Road. No. 1143 (XUF 143) is seen here in 1973, resplendent in traditional green livery. This 1960-built Leyland Leopard had beautiful Weymann coachwork that would seat just thirty-seven passengers. A selection of 'Queen Mary' double-deckers is also visible.

Southdown's distinctive Queen Mary Leyland PD3/4 fully-fronted double-deckers were almost as famous as London's AEC Routemasters. Most were bodied by Northern Counties, such as this fine example, No. 424 (424 DCD), which is seen in open-top configuration. This vehicle was in fact convertible and in winter months the sixty-nine seated passengers would have a roof over their heads. The bus is photographed in preservation days at a rally in Netley Park near Southampton in July 1990.

Later deliveries of double-decker buses to Southdown consisted of standard NBC vehicles in corporate green colours. An early example was No. 2101 (OCD 771G), which was delivered in 1969. This Bristol VRT/SL6G with the earlier style of ECW bodywork, seating seventy, is seen in the yard of Provincial's Hoeford depot in 1981.

It is a dull day in central Portsmouth in March 1981. The city's famous Guildhall looms over Southdown No. 613 (UWV 613S), a Bristol VRT/SL3/6LXB that was built in 1978. With ECW bodywork capable of conversion to open-top, its roof remains firmly in place on this cold day.

The mid-1980s saw Southdown being given a little freedom in its choice of livery in the run up to privatisation. A version of the old colour scheme was re-introduced and has been applied to No. 648 (AAP 648T) – another Bristol VRT/SL3/6LXB with ECW seventy-four-seat bodywork. It is seen in a busy Havant bus station in the summer of 1986.

Also photographed in the summer of 1986 is Southdown No. 1322 (BWV 922T), which is a Leyland Leopard/Plaxton Supreme Express forty-eight-seat coach that has been painted into an unusual version of the coach livery. The location is by the Eastern Docks in Southampton. Southdown sold out to the Stagecoach Group in 1989.

After deregulation, the Isle of Wight operator Southern Vectis, being unable to expand due to its island confines, decided to cross the water and begin bus services in the Southampton area. A two-tone blue and yellow livery was adopted for these operations, which went under the name of Solent Blue Line. In the first summer of operation, 1987, No. 66 (GNJ 566N) is seen in central Southampton. This Bristol VRT/SL6G with seventy-four-seat ECW bodywork had been new to Southdown in 1974.

In September 1989, Solent Blue Line No. 433 (JTH 760P) is seen in Vincent's Walk in Southampton city centre. New to South Wales Transport in 1975, this Leyland National saloon was originally capable of seating fifty-two passengers.

Many of Solent Blue Line's services were actually operated by buses owned by Marchwood Motorways of Totton, just outside Southampton. Included in that fleet was No. 502 (F246 RJX). This DAF SB220 with forty-seven-seat Optare Delta bodywork, new in 1989, is seen about to leave Bargate Street in the city centre in September of that year.

New to Solent Blue Line (though registered in the Isle of Wight), No. 211 (G211 YDL), a Mercedes 811D/Phoenix thirty-one-seat minibus, is seen in Vincent's Walk, Southampton, in the summer of 1990. This bus later saw service with Wilfreda-Beehive in Doncaster.

Photographed next to Ford Transit minibus No. 226 at Eastleigh depot in summer 1990 is Solent Blue Line No. 201 (LFJ 849W). This 7-foot 6-inch-wide, thirty-five-seat Bristol LHS6L – bodied by ECW – had been new to Western National, where it would have been well-suited to the country lanes of Devon and Cornwall.

Another Marchwood Motorways bus in Solent Blue Line colours, No. 214 (H712 LOL) is seen in Bargate Street, Southampton, in 1991, only a few months after it had been delivered. The vehicle is a Dennis Dart with Carlyle bodywork, capable of seating forty-two passengers.

Solent Blue Line's No. 700 (A700 DDL) had been transferred to the mainland from the parent company, Southern Vectis. This 1984-built Leyland Olympian with seventy-seven-seat ECW bodywork is seen in central Southampton in 1991 under the control of a brave traffic warden and passing the old Cannon Cinema in a street known as Above Bar.

The larger type of minibus was still a popular concept in the mid-1990s. Solent Blue Line was no exception to this trend and an example of this type is illustrated here in Southampton City Centre (Hanover Buildings) in the summer of 1994. The vehicle, No. 241 (M241 XPO), an Iveco/Fiat 59-12 with bodywork by European Coach Conversions that was capable of seating twenty-nine passengers, had been new a few months earlier.

Another Marchwood Motorways bus to bear Solent Blue Line's colours was No. 505 (L510 EHD). Bought new by the company in 1993, the DAF SB220/Ikarus B48F saloon is seen in Bargate Street, Southampton, in the summer of 1994.

Solent Blue Line No. 526 (L526 YDL) is seen loading up outside the Southampton branch of the Birmingham Midshires Building Society on a street named Hanover Buildings, summer 1994. This Volvo B10B-58, with Alexander 'Strider' fifty-one-seat body, had been new to the company earlier in the year.

Solent Blue Line No. 557 (R557 UOT), a Dennis Dart SLF with forty-four-seat UVG bodywork, was another of those Marchwood Motorways buses to wear the blue and yellow livery. One of the first low-floor vehicles, it was photographed on Pound Tree Road in Southampton city centre in autumn 1998.

With seventy high-backed seats for coaching duties, Solent Blue Line No. 736 (M736 BBP) had been new to the company in 1995. The East Lancs-bodied Volvo Olympian is seen alongside part of the city walls in Bargate Street, Southampton, in the autumn of 1995.

By 1999 the low-floor double-decker had arrived with Solent Blue Line and No. 743 (T743 JPO) is seen in October of the following year on the edge of Southampton City Centre, heading for Winchester. That is an appropriate destination for a vehicle named *Spirit of King Alfred*, which was a Dennis Trident with East Lancs H47/27F bodywork.

In 2003, Solent Blue Line began to be rebranded as Blue Star and two years later became part of the Go Ahead Group. In March 2006, No. 753 (HX51 ZRE) is seen arriving at Eastleigh bus station in its new colours. This seventy-three-seat Volvo B7TL with East Lancs bodywork had been delivered new in December 2001.

Sister vehicle to the one shown in the lower picture of page XX, No. 775 (T745 JPO), originally numbered 745, is seen in its new Blue Star livery. It is photographed outside Swaythling railway station, north of Southampton, on 12 May 2010.

Solent Blue Line/Blue Star today operates the Unilink services on behalf of Southampton University. Bus No. 1556 (HJ63 JMU) – an Alexander Dennis E40D Enviro double-decker, fitted with dual-doorway and sixty-five-seats – is seen loading up in Castle Way, Southampton, on 8 July 2014. Another Blue Star bus – a Mercedes saloon – is having a rest behind.

The first street tramways in the city of Portsmouth were horse-operated and opened in 1874. The system gradually expanded and was taken over in 1901 by Portsmouth Corporation, who quickly electrified the city's network. By 1911, the business owned 100 trams. At about that time, No. 91 – a typical open-top car of the era – is seen passing through floodwater, which is filling the dip below Portsmouth & Southsea railway station. Note the instruction to passengers: 'Keep your seats while passing under the bridge'.

Portsmouth's trams were replaced by trolleybuses between 1934 and 1936. At the same spot as the previous photograph we see trolleybus No. 228 (RV 8310) in around 1960. This Cravens-bodied AEC 661T fifty-two-seater had been part of a large batch delivered new in 1936. The railway bridge now holds an advert for 'Sunshine Ale', brewed by Brickwood's, which was based in the city. Trolleybus operation ceased in 1963. Photograph by the late Les Flint.

Back in the 1970s, Portsmouth was very much 'Atlantean City', with a fleet of such vehicles that were supplemented with some single-deck buses. Typical of the Leyland Atlanteans of the time, Portsmouth City Transport No. 207 (207 BTP) – a PDR1/1 built in 1963 with Metro-Cammell seventy-six-seat bodywork – is seen in Commercial Road in the city centre beside the Albany Bars pub in 1973.

Sister vehicle to the one in the photograph above, Portsmouth City Transport No. 222 (222 BTP) is seen at the appropriate stop beside what is now the Hard Interchange, beside Portsmouth Harbour railway station and ferry terminals, around 1975.

Prior to the arrival of the Atlanteans, Portsmouth City Transport had favoured the Leyland Titan PD2/12 as the standard vehicle for main line service within the city. Several were retained and converted to open-top for tourist duties. One of these, No. 2 (LRV 992), is seen departing from Southsea Pier in 1976, heading for Hayling Ferry on the seafront service. Built in 1956 and originally given fleet number 100, the bus carries Metro-Cammell bodywork, with a fifty-six-passenger seating capacity when new.

New to Portsmouth City Transport as No. 94 (LRV 986) and identical to the one pictured above, this Leyland PD2/12 has been converted to open-top and renumbered as 5. It is photographed at the Hard waiting for departure time on the seafront service in the year of Her Majesty the Queen's Silver Jubilee, 1977, while suitably decorated for the occasion.

The rear-loading Leyland Titans of Portsmouth City Transport were later replaced by Atlanteans, which were also converted to open-top. No. 9 (ERV 250D), a 1966-built PDR1/1 with MCW bodywork, is seen on its stance at the Hard in 1981. When new it had been numbered 250 and had a seating capacity of seventy-six.

Portsmouth City Transport No. 163, a Leyland Panther Cub bodied by MCW, is seen at the Hard around 1975. The bus had been built in 1967, with forty-two seats and a dual-doorway layout. To the rear is Atlantean No. 207, which is stood in front of Portsmouth Harbour station's signal box.

Another type of single-deck bus in the Portsmouth City Transport fleet was the AEC Swift, such as this one, No. 185 (NTP 185H). Seating forty-two passengers in a dual-doored Marshall body, it is seen on a wet day at the Hard around 1975.

For its principal fleet, Portsmouth City Transport continued to buy Leyland Atlanteans during the 1970s. No. 264 (VTP 264L), an AN68/1R type with Alexander H45/30D bodywork that was new in 1972, is seen around 1976 at Southsea Pier next to a Whitbread pub, a shellfish stall and, for some reason, a United Counties dual-purpose Bristol RE.

Deliveries of the Leyland Atlantean PDR1/1R buses with Alexander bodywork for Portsmouth City Transport were frequent throughout the 1970s, with the last ones being received in 1979. Part of the 1973 batch, No. 291 (VTP 291L) is seen at the Hard around 1975 alongside two fine Brickwood's pubs (by then owned by Whitbread) – the King & Queen and the Ship Anson. In 1987, the two hostelries were combined into one.

The AEC Swifts and Leyland Panther Cubs purchased by Portsmouth City Transport did not find favour and therefore, in 1976, fourteen dual-door Leyland National thirty-eight-seaters were purchased. One of these, No. 103 (KCR 103P), is seen awaiting departure time and passengers at the Hard in 1981.

The last batch of Leyland Atlanteans (345 – 354) for Portsmouth City Transport were delivered in 1980 and were of the AN68/1R specification, with dual-door bodywork by East Lancs that was capable of seating seventy-three passengers. No. 348 (CPO 348W) is seen at the Hard on a sunny day in 1982.

1982 saw the delivery to Portsmouth City Transport of three unusual Dennis Lancets with locally built Wadham Stringer bodywork. One was a dual-purpose thirty-three-seater, but the other two, including No. 97 (GTP 97X), was a service bus, seating thirty-five. It is seen in 1986 having just passed beneath Portsmouth & Southsea railway station, with the Guildhall prominent behind.

Portsmouth City Transport was privatised in 1988, being sold to its employees and Southampton Citybus as a joint venture that was named Portsmouth Citybus. No. 321 (UOR 321T), another AN68A/1R bodied by Alexander, is seen in its new colours at the Hard on a wet day in early 1989. Later in that year, Portsmouth Citybus was sold to the Stagecoach Group.

The former Portsmouth City Transport operations, in Stagecoach hands, became known as Southdown Portsmouth (Stagecoach had already taken over Southdown). Bearing that fleet name and Stagecoach's famous stripes, No. 316 (KSA 182P) is seen at the Hard in early 1991. A typical Portsmouth vehicle at first glance, the Scottish registration reveals that this Alexander-bodied Leyland Atlantean AN68/1R had been new to Grampian Regional Transport in Aberdeen. Soon after this photograph was taken, Southdown Portsmouth was sold on to Transit Holdings.

Transit Holdings, the owners of Devon General, soon made their mark on services in Portsmouth by introducing minibus services using the name Blue Admiral. Proudly displaying its new livery is ex-Devon General No. 805 (E805 WDV), a sixteen-seat Ford Transit with Mellor bodywork. It is seen in Southsea in mid-1991.

The dual-doored minibus later came to Blue Admiral. No. 2061 (L313 BOD) is an Iveco/Fiat 59.12, again with Mellor bodywork, that can seat twenty-six passengers. It is seen alongside a similar bus of People's Provincial at the Hard Interchange, Portsmouth, in autumn 1995. The next year, Transit Holdings' operations in Portsmouth were sold to First Group. We will take a look at that organisation's Hampshire business later, after examining Southampton's municipal buses, which met the same fate.

The Southampton Tramways Company began operations in the city in 1879, using horse traction. The business was compulsory purchased by Southampton Corporation in 1898. Electrification began two years later and eventually a considerable network was operated. The winter of 1908 saw some terrible weather and Southampton city centre was badly affected, but the trams continued to run, as seen here, though nobody seems to want to use the open top deck!

Southampton Corporation Transport gradually modernised the tram fleet, building their own bodies to enable them to pass through the restricted height of the Bargate, which car No. 6 is about to negotiate. Similar tram No. 11 is on the avoiding curve, dating the photograph to between 1932 and 1938. The Southampton tram system ceased operating in 1949. The Bargate survives today, though road traffic no longer passes through.

By the early 1970s, Southampton City Transport's bus fleet consisted mainly of Leyland PD2 types or AEC Regent V double-deckers. Typical of the period is this PD2/27 with rather angular Park Royal bodywork, seating sixty-six passengers. No. 304 (304 TR), delivered in 1961, is seen in Vincent's Walk in 1973. This is right in the city centre, but is bordered by the green area known as Houndwell Park.

Nearly identical Park Royal bodywork was fitted to the 1962 batch of AEC Regent V buses, such as No. 314 (314 AOW), which is again seen in Vincent's Walk, this time sometime around 1975. Behind is No. 327 (327 AOW), another Park Royal-bodied bus that is this time on a Leyland PD2A/27 chassis.

The 1966 delivery of AEC Regent V buses to Southampton City Transport differed from earlier buses in that they had seventy-seat bodywork by Neepsend Coachworks of Sheffield. No. 379 (HCR 136D) is seen in 1976 heading towards the railway station and Royal Pier on West Park Road.

Southampton City Transport had a small fleet of single-deck buses for the less demanding duties. No. 2 (MTR 420F), an AEC Swift with Strachans B47D bodywork, is seen on the open-air inspection pit at the main depot in Portswood, to the north of the city centre, in 1977. No. 2 was withdrawn later that year.

In addition to the AEC Swifts, Southampton City Transport purchased five Seddon RU saloons in 1972, all of which were forty-four-seaters bodied by Pennine. Seen at the depot yard in 1977 is No. 13 (BCR 377K), which was withdrawn in 1981.

The East Lancs-bodied Leyland Atlantean became the standard double-deck bus for Southampton City Transport, with deliveries starting in 1968. The last batch were received in 1982, one of which is seen here. No. 272 (KOW 272Y), an AN68C/1R with a seventy-six-seat body, was photographed in its original colours on Vincent's Walk, central Southampton, in the summer of 1986.

Southampton City Transport was not totally immune to the minibus craze of the mid-1980s. No. 50 (D50 ERV) is seen in Portswood in April 1987, only a few months after delivery. This Iveco/Fiat 49.10 had a Robin Hood body capable of seating twenty-one passengers. Note that the fleet name had now changed to Southampton Citybus.

Another trend during the mid-to late 1980s was to buy former London AEC Routemaster buses. Southampton Citybus was no exception and No. 408 (713 DYE) is seen on Vincent's Walk in the city centre in September 1987. This Park Royal-bodied bus had been new to London Transport as No. RM1713 in 1963.

Southampton City Transport purchased one Dennis Dominator in 1984 and Southampton Citybus received a small batch of four more – bodied by East Lancs – in 1986. Seating seventy-six passengers, No. 281 (C281 BBP) is seen beside the rear door of Marks & Spencer on Vincent's Walk in the spring of 1987.

Further East Lancs-bodied Dennis Dominators followed. No. 296 (F296 PTP), with a different body style, was delivered to Southampton Citybus in 1989. This seventy-six-seat bus is seen in the all-over red colour scheme in Vincent's Walk, September 1989.

In 1986 Southampton Citybus purchased four Leyland Olympians fitted with coach seating. Providing comfort for the customers heading to Lords Hill, a suburb of the city, is No. 286 (C286 BBP), which is seen at Vincent's Walk in the summer of 1989. Bodywork is by East Lancs, which is capable of seating seventy passengers.

In the later years of Southampton Citybus, single-deck buses were ordered in much greater numbers. This Leyland Lynx saloon had forty-seven dual-purpose seats and is being used on an appropriate duty: the 727 express route to Portsmouth. No. 112 (G112 XOW) was photographed on Pound Tree Road in central Southampton in mid-1991.

Southampton Citybus was sold to its employees in 1993, though things remained without change from the view of the general public. Single-deck bus No. 114 (K114 PRV) was photographed on Vincent's Walk in autumn 1995. Originally a demonstrator, this Volvo B10-58 with Northern Counties fifty-one-seat bodywork had been new in 1993.

Another ex-demonstrator in the Southampton Citybus fleet was No. 115 (M967 GDU). This had been new to body manufacturer Plaxton's of Scarborough as an example of that company's 'Verde' model, which seated fifty-one passengers. With a Volvo B10-58 chassis, it is seen in Vincent's Walk, Southampton, in late 1995.

Southampton Citybus No. 351 (OJI 1871) started life as an East Lancs-bodied double-deck Leyland Atlantean AN68/1R of 1975 vintage, then registered as HTR 567P. It was rebodied by East Lancs to become a thirty-five-seat saloon in 1991. As such, it was photographed at Southampton Central railway station in mid-1992 while operating the shuttle service to the Red Funnel ferry terminal.

Yet another single-deck bus, No. 307 (G895 XPX) was a Dennis Dart thirty-three-seater that had been new as a demonstrator. New to Wadham Stringer, Waterlooville, Hampshire, a bodywork builder, in 1990, it is seen in Southampton Citybus livery at Vincent's Walk in mid-1991.

An unusual vehicle to join the Southampton Citybus was No. 504. It had been re-registered WLT 649 and was originally carried by an AEC Routemaster of London Transport. New to London Coaches as No. LC1 (C201 DYE), this coach-seated Leyland Olympian/East Lancs seventy-seater is seen just outside Southampton city centre in the autumn of 1992 while bearing 'Red Ensign' markings for coaching duties.

Despite being heavily rebuilt after the bombing of the Second World War, many historic buildings still survive in central Southampton, making it worthwhile for Southampton Citybus to operate an open-top sightseeing tour in conjunction with Guide Friday of Stratford-upon-Avon. Painted in the latter's livery, but also with Citybus labelling, is former Southampton City Transport No. 139 (WOW 529J) – a Leyland Atlantean PDR1A/1, bodied by East Lancs and converted to become roofless. It is seen passing Burger King – which is not necessarily one of the city's main tourist attractions – in Bargate Street, in the summer of 1994.

The 727 (later renumbered 747) express service between Southampton and Portsmouth became jointly operated by Southampton Citybus and Stagecoach South Coast. A coach belonging to the latter is seen on such duties bearing Citybus markings in Pound Tree Avenue, Southampton, in autumn 1995. This vehicle is a Dennis Javelin with Plaxton forty-seven-seat coachwork, numbered 1105 and registered M103 CCD. It later went elsewhere within the Stagecoach Group and ended up with Cresswell of Broadway, Worcestershire.

Southampton Citybus No. 305 (G305 XCR) was new in 1990 as a conventional thirty-five-seat Dennis Dart/Carlyle saloon. It was later converted to run on gas, as seen in this photograph taken on Vincent's Walk in autumn 1995.

A second-hand purchase by Southampton Citybus was that of No. 126 (STK 126T), a former Plymouth Leyland Atlantean AN68A/1R with Roe bodywork. It retained the same fleet number (matching the registration) throughout its life in both fleets. Here it is seen in the city centre at its Vincent's Walk stance in late 1995, contrasting nicely with the more conventional (for Southampton) East Lancs-bodied Atlantean behind.

Southampton Citybus No. 294 (P294 KPX) was delivered new in September 1996 in all-over white. It retained this livery for a few months, as seen when photographed here on Vincent's Walk six months later. Northern Counties seventy-seven-seat bodywork is fitted to a Volvo Olympian chassis.

In July 1997 the Southampton Citybus business was sold to First Group. First Group's famous 'f' symbol was soon applied, though the red livery was retained for a while, as seen applied to No. 269 (FTR 269X). This bus had been part of the penultimate batch of East Lancs-bodied Leyland Atlantean AN68C/1R double-deckers that were delivered to Southampton City Transport in 1981. It is seen in Pound Tree Avenue in late 1998.

The low-floor single-decker came to Southampton Citybus just before the First Group takeover. Delivered in 1996, this Dennis Dart SLF with Plaxton thirty-seven-seat bodywork, No. 405 (P405 KOW), is seen with its Firstbus identity in Pound Tree Avenue towards the end of 1998.

Transfers within the First Group became commonplace, meaning a repaint usually became necessary prior to any re-entry into service. Such a fate befell First Southampton No. 524 (JHE 144W), an MCW Metrobus transferred from the company's Yorkshire operations. It had been new as South Yorkshire PTE No. 1844 in 1981 and was photographed in Pound Tree Avenue in autumn 2000.

First Group also purchased the business of People's Provincial in 1995, adopting a red and cream livery, as displayed by Leyland National No. 313 (JBP 131P), which is seen leaving Gosport bus station in early 1997. This forty-four-seat, dual-doored example had been new to Provincial as No. 31 in 1975.

In this photograph, taken around 1998, First Provincial's red and cream colour scheme is applied, but only First Group's corporate identity is displayed. No. 408 (MDS 867V), a Leyland National 2 saloon, is seen in Southampton's High Street. This vehicle had been new to Scottish operator Central SMT in 1980.

On the same occasion as above, First Provincial No. 167 (L167 TRV) is mainly decorated in an advert for an electronics company with branches in Portsmouth and Waterlooville, but not Southampton! This twenty-seven-seat Marshall-bodied Fiat/Iveco 59.12 had been new to Provincial in 1994.

Another minibus carrying First Provincial livery, No. 727 (P727 KCR) is seen on a sunny summer's day in 2000 entering Havant's bus station. Purchased new by Provincial in 1996, it is a Mercedes 709D with Plaxton bodywork capable of seating twenty-seven passengers.

The advantages of a national corporate identity, when buses move between fleets, are seen to good effect in Gosport bus station in March 2003. The old colour scheme is still applied to the two minibuses and the Provincial fleet name has now vanished. Having been transferred from elsewhere in the Firstbus empire, fleet number 1091 (H641 YHT) has the latest livery. This Leyland Lynx saloon had been new to the Bristol Omnibus Company as a forty-nine-seat bus in 1990.

Southampton's 'City Link' service, connecting the main railway station with the central area and the quays, was operated by First Hampshire using this twenty-seven-seat Optare Solo. No. 733 (X733 FPO) is seen heading south along Castle Way in autumn 2000.

In October 2000, the date of this photograph, Firstbus had introduced the company's 'Barbie' livery, seen applied to No. 138 (X138 FPO). This articulated Volvo B7LA with Wright fifty-six-seat, dual-door bodywork is seen in Pound Tree Avenue, Southampton. At the time, local fleet names were still in use and the five-figure national numbering scheme had not yet been introduced.

First Group's 'Barbie' livery began to be phased out from 2012 in order to be replaced by this new scheme, which incorporated local logos for each area. 'Southampton' is clearly applied to No. 32043 (W813 EOW), a Volvo B7TL with Alexander bodywork seating seventy-eight passengers. It had been new as First Hampshire No. 813 in 2000. The bus is seen leaving Bargate Street in Southampton on 8 July 2014.

Firstbus No. 69243 (YJ07 WFM) is also seen in Southampton city centre passing along the High Street on 8 July 2014. Very much a standard vehicle for the company, this forty-four-seat Wright-bodied Volvo B7RLE differs from the norm by having the sides of the bus covered in advertising for a local travel website.

Southampton's bus route number 3, run by First Hampshire, is operated by Volvo B7RLE/Wright saloons that are painted in a dedicated red livery. No. 69390 (HY09 AOS) was photographed en route from Lords Hill to Thornhill on 8 July 2014 when it was about to enter the High Street in the city centre.

Firstbus is also now the dominant operator in Portsmouth. The company's Barbie livery is seen applied to No. 42234 (T34 JCV), a Dennis Dart SLF with Plaxton bodywork. Though looking very much like a standard First Group vehicle, the bus had, in fact, been new to Cornish operator Truronian, which had been bought by First in 2008. This photograph was taken on Edinburgh Road, in the heart of Portsmouth city centre, on 22 October 2014.

Above: The high-frequency service between Portsmouth and Waterlooville is operated by Firstbus using 'The Star' branding and an appropriately sparkling colour scheme. A fleet of integral Wright Streetlite DF forty-one-seat saloons is used, an example being No. 63062 (SK63 KKC), which is seen on Edinburgh Road, Portsmouth, on 22 October 2014.

Below: Another First vehicle in a dedicated livery is No. 33896 (SN14 TRV), an Alexander Dennis Enviro double-decker seating seventy-four passengers. It is operating the Park and Ride service from a site close to the M275 motorway, north of the city centre, to its terminus at the Hard Interchange, where it was photographed on 22 October 2014.

Despite the loss of the two municipal bus operators in Hampshire, one council-owned route still runs into the county. Reading Transport, under the guise of Newbury Buses, operates an hourly service from Newbury (Berkshire), via Kingsclere, to Basingstoke. On such duties, No. 501 (RX07 RKV) is seen outside Basingstoke railway station on 12 May 2010. This is a rare MAN 18.240 with East Lancs H50/29F bodywork, which is wearing a dedicated livery for the route, marketed as 'The Link'.

For a time, Accord Operations ran the free shuttle service between Southampton Central railway station and the city's quays. The 'Town Quay' is, of course, where the ferries to Hythe and the Isle of Wight depart from, but the West Quay is a shopping centre. In September 2006, No. 51 (PE55 WPP) is seen here. This dual-doored East Lancs-bodied Alexander Dennis Dart SLF seating twenty-nine passengers had been purchased new earlier in 2006.

Accord Operations also ran the 'Uni-Link' network, which mainly carried students around the university campuses in Southampton. On such duties, No. 33 (YN04 YJT) is seen just north of the city centre on 17 August 2007. Another dual-doored bus, it is an East Lancs-bodied Scania N94UD. The University of Southampton's bus services have since passed to Go Ahead subsidiary Blue Star.

Portsmouth University also runs bus services for its students. One of its vehicles is KX59 GNU, an Alexander Dennis Enviro capable of seating eighty passengers. It is seen on Winston Churchill Avenue, just south of the city centre, on 22 October 2014. This bus has since passed to Reading Buses.

Emsworth & District have been operating buses in South East Hampshire and West Sussex since the 1970s. Their green vehicles are a common sight in Havant bus station, where G778 WFC was found in August 2000. This Optare Metrorider was delivered new to City of Oxford Motor Services as a twenty-three-seat bus in 1990.

Also seen in Havant bus station on that sunny August day in 2000 is Emsworth & District G767 CDU. Though the front of the bus has been painted in the correct colours, the rest of the bus still carries a reminder of its previous owners, as it is promoting the delights of Burnley Market! Though this Reeve Burgess-bodied Leyland Swift had been new as a demonstrator, it had spent most of its life with Hyndburn Transport in Accrington, Lancashire.

Arriving at Havant bus station on 8 February 2008 is Emsworth & District-owned J505 GCD. This Dennis Dart with forty-one-seat Alexander Dash bodywork had been new to another South Coast operator – Stagecoach, in Hastings.

Emsworth is a small town situated very close to Hampshire's border with West Sussex. Basil Williams of that location traded under the name of Southern Motorways. At the depot in the summer of 1986, we see an interesting collection of vehicles. The Plaxton-bodied Ford R1114, JNK 994N, had been bought new in 1975, but the buses lined up behind were all second-hand. NTP179H and NTP186H, on the right, were AEC Swifts with dual-door Marshall bodywork new to Portsmouth Corporation in 1969. To the left of that couple can be seen JRT 81K, another AEC Swift, which was bodied by Willowbrook and originally ran with Ipswich Corporation.

Southern Motorways later became known as Hants & Sussex and were well known for their fleet of former London Transport AEC Swifts (or Merlins as they were called in the capital). One example was AML 80H, which was originally a dual-doored bus bodied by Park Royal and registered SMS 80 when new. Seen after conversion to single-door, it was photographed beside the Queens Hotel in Southsea in mid-1991.

Hants & Sussex survived until the company went out of business in the 1990s. The AEC Swifts had become increasingly unreliable and the company resorted to dealerships to supply serviceable buses. On such was M822 RCP, a DAF SB220 with Northern Counties bodywork, which is seen approaching Havant bus station in autumn 1995. By 2000 this vehicle had passed to a Manchester operator called UK North.

Above: The vehicles of a Berkshire operator, Courtney of Bracknell, can often be seen in North Hampshire. In a special livery for Basingstoke & Deane Council, KX08 HME is seen passing Basingstoke railway station on 12 May 2010. This Alexander Dennis Enviro saloon, seating twenty-nine passengers, had been new to the company in early 2008.

Below: A local coach operator, Home James Coach Travel of Southampton, ventured into the stage-carriage market for a short while. An ex-Brighton Dennis Dominator, bodied by East Lancs, OAP 16W was used on these duties. It was photographed on Pound Tree Road, in the city centre, in late 1998.

Within the Borough of Eastleigh is the village of West End, where Princess Coaches have their base. Founded in 1919, the company today concentrates on private hire and school work. For a short while Princess Coaches operated the City Clipper bus services in Southampton, on which duties MX07 BAU is seen arriving at Southampton Central railway station on 17 August 2007. The company had bought this Plaxton Primo twenty-eight-seat bus new earlier in 2007.

Altonian Coaches was a long-established coach company based in the lovely Hampshire town of Alton. The company's depot was close to the railway station. Sometime around 1975, one of the firm's oldest vehicles is seen in the depot yard awaiting restoration. GOU 596 had been new to Altonian in 1949 as a thirty-three-seat, Scottish Aviation-bodied Tilling Stevens K6MA7. This vehicle has since been restored to operational condition.

Oakley Services – a coach company based at the village of the same name, a few miles west of Basingstoke – ran an interesting collection of vehicles in the 1990s. Seen in March 1993 in the outskirts of Basingstoke is D213 MKK, a Scania K92CRS with East Lancs bodywork. It had been new as a ninety-two seater (!) for Maidstone Boro'line in 1987.

At Oakley Services' depot, also in March 1993, we see a former West Midlands PTE bus, alongside other vehicles in the fleet. GOG 533N, a Daimler Fleetline with Park Royal seventy-six-seat bodywork, had been numbered 4533 during its time around Birmingham.

Marchwood Motorways, as well as operating buses on behalf of Solent Blue Line, also undertook duties using their own name. For several years, the company ran the service connecting Southampton Central railway station with the Red Funnel ferries from a quay near the Eastern Docks. Sometime around 1975, at Southampton Central railway station, is EHO 10K, a Ford R192 with Duple Viceroy Express forty-five-seat coachwork. Alongside is VOT 410H, a Plaxton-bodied Bedford SB5. At the time, Marchwood Motorways also ran buses in far-flung West Wales!

An unusual bus to wear Marchwood Motorways livery was W232 CDN, fleet number 821, which is seen on a contract duty for P&O Ferries near Southampton Central railway station on 17 August 2007. This DAF DE02/Optare Spectra double-decker had been new to the company in 2000.

Maybury's Coaches of Cranbourne, Dorset, no longer trade, but back in 1987 had taken advantage of deregulation and were operating stage-carriage services. In September of that year, former London Buses No. DMS1962 (KUC 962P) – a Daimler Fleetline/MCW combination – was photographed on Castle Way in Southampton. It will soon be departing for Lymington.

Sometime in the spring of 1987, Maybury's Coaches-owned EJF 17T has just arrived on the number 56 service from Lymington at Southampton's bus station. This Bedford YMT with fifty-three-seat Unicar coach bodywork had been new to Ralph's Coaches of Longford, West London. In July 1987, the bus station in Southampton was closed for redevelopment.

Countryliner, a Sussex-based company, went into administration in 2012. Prior to that it had operated a large amount of bus services within its home county and into Surrey and part of Hampshire. On Lavant Street in Petersfield, T78 JBA is photographed on 11 September 2008. This Dennis Dart SLF/Plaxton bus had been new to Scottish operator Davidson of Bathgate as a twenty-nine-seat bus.

Countywide Travel was formed in 1995 from a base in Basingstoke. Several services were operated, including into Berkshire. However, it is close to Basingstoke's railway station that we see M71 AKA in the summer of 2002. This forty-seat Dennis Dart, bodied by Marshall, had been new to Halton Transport, from Widnes, Cheshire. Countywide Travel was sold to Stagecoach towards the end of 2011.

Above: Brijan Tours was established in the early 1990s and operated several services in South Hampshire. At Petersfield, approaching the railway station on 11 September 2008, we see G505 VYE. This twenty-eight-seat Dennis Dart/Carlyle saloon had been delivered to London Buses in 1990.

Below: Another bus that had seen service in the capital was No. 112 (PUI 8112) in the Brijan Tours fleet. This Alexander 'Dash'-bodied Dennis Dart had been new as N318 AMC, a thirty-six-seater with Stagecoach East London. It is seen arriving at Eastleigh bus station on 10 July 2014. Brijan Tours ceased trading a year later.

Black Velvet Travel, trading as Velvet, began life in 2007 and started operating bus services in the next year from its headquarters in Eastleigh. At the height of its operation, the company ran several routes around its home town and into the nearby city of Southampton. At Eastleigh bus station, on 12 May 2010, J843 TSC is preparing for departure. This Leyland Olympian/ Alexander R-type double-decker had been new as a dual-doored bus with Lothian Buses in Edinburgh.

As part of the Velvet fleet, R258 KRG, a Volvo B10BLE with forty-four-seat Alexander bodywork, had been new to Stagecoach's Busways operation in Newcastle-upon-Tyne. It is seen in Bargate Street, Southampton, beside part of the city's walls on 8 July 2014. Eight days later the company announced that it had ceased trading, though services resumed after a gap of just a couple of days. Bus operations finally ceased in January 2015.

Xelabus is another independent based in the railway town of Eastleigh and running stage-carriage services around that area. The company was founded as recently as 2010 and has established a firm presence in the local bus scene. The company's green livery is seen applied to J12 XEL (named *Phoebe*), which is a Dennis Trident with Alexander ALX 400 bodywork, as it enters Eastleigh's small bus station on 10 July 2014. The bus had been new as No. TA100 (T218 CLO) in the fleet of Metroline in London.

On the same occasion, taking a rest at Eastleigh bus station, is Xelabus YT11 LPZ, which has been given fleet number 415. This forty-two-seat all-Scania K23OU84 had been purchased from Menzies of Heathrow, where it had operated services in and around the airport. At the time of writing, Xelabus are still operating buses and will hopefully continue to do so for many more years.